TOP TEN CHALLENGES FOR INDIE/SELF-PUBLISHED AUTHORS

B Alan Bourgeois

AWARD-WINNING AUTHOR
AWARD-WINNING SPEAKER
AUTHOR ADVOCATE

NAVIGATING THE ROAD TO SUCCESS

B Alan Bourgeois

Top Ten Challenges for Indie/Self-Published Authors: Navigating the Road to Success

© B Alan Bourgeois 2023

All rights reserved. No part of this publication may be reproduced, stored in a retrieval system, or transmitted in any form or by any means, electronic, mechanical, photocopying, recording, or otherwise, without the prior written permission of the publisher.

The information and opinions expressed in this book are believed to be accurate and reliable, but no responsibility or liability is assumed by the publisher for any errors, omissions, or any damages caused by the use of these products, procedures, or methods presented herein.

The book is sold and distributed on an "as is" basis without warranties of any kind, either expressed or implied, including but not limited to warranties of merchantability or fitness for a particular purpose. The purchaser or reader of this book assumes complete responsibility for the use of these materials and information.

Any legal disputes arising from the use of this book shall be governed by the laws of the jurisdiction where the book was purchased, without regard to its conflict of law provisions, and shall be resolved exclusively in the courts of that jurisdiction.

ISBN: 978-1-0880-9060-2

Publisher: Bourgeois Media & Consulting (BourgeoisMedia.com)

Introduction

Are you an indie author with a fire in your heart and a story to share? Do you dream of navigating the ever-evolving landscape of self-publishing, where the competition is fierce, but the possibilities are endless? If your answer is a resounding "yes," then you've embarked on a thrilling journey that's filled with promise and potential. Welcome to the realm of indie publishing, where creativity knows no bounds, and authors like you are forging new paths every day.

In this vast and often challenging world of self-publishing, we understand that you face obstacles unique to your craft. But remember this: every challenge is an opportunity in disguise, a chance to learn, grow, and emerge stronger. With the right guidance, determination, and a dash of courage, you can conquer the hurdles that lie ahead. That's where "Top Ten Challenges for Indie/Self-Published Authors" comes into play, your trusted companion on this exciting expedition.

Within the pages of this indispensable guide, you'll discover a treasure trove of insights and strategies to help you surmount the obstacles that indie authors commonly encounter. From finding your audience to mastering the art of marketing, from establishing credibility to ensuring the quality of your work, we're here to equip you with the knowledge and tools to rise above the challenges.

But remember, these challenges are not insurmountable; they are stepping stones on your path to indie publishing success. So, join us as we dive into each of these ten challenges, armed with hope, determination, and the unwavering belief that your story deserves to be heard. Your journey as an indie author begins now, and it's a journey filled with boundless potential. Let's embark on this adventure together.

Contents

1. **Finding an Audience**: One of the biggest challenges for indie authors is reaching and connecting with their target audience. Without the backing of a traditional publishing house, it can be challenging to gain visibility and attract readers.   6

2. **Limited Marketing Resources**: Indie authors often have limited financial resources for marketing and promoting their books. They need to find effective and affordable ways to market their books, such as utilizing social media, book blogs, and online book communities.   9

3. **Building Credibility**: Without the validation of a traditional publishing house, indie authors may struggle to establish credibility and gain the trust of readers. Building a strong author brand and receiving positive reviews and endorsements can help overcome this challenge.   12

4. **Quality Control**: Self-published authors are responsible for editing, proofreading, and formatting their books. Ensuring high-quality content and a professional presentation can be challenging without the guidance and support of traditional publishing professionals.   15

5. **Distribution and Bookstores**: Getting self-published books into brick-and-mortar bookstores can be difficult, as many stores prefer to carry books from established publishers. Limited distribution options can hinder the visibility and availability of self-published books.   18

6. **Financial Considerations**: Indie authors often face financial challenges, as they bear the costs of editing, cover   21

design, marketing, and other publishing expenses. Generating sufficient income from book sales can be a challenge, especially for new and unknown authors.

7. **Time Management**: Self-publishing requires authors to handle all aspects of the publishing process, from writing and editing to marketing and distribution. Balancing these responsibilities with other obligations and commitments can be overwhelming and time-consuming. 24

8. **Overcoming Stigma**: Despite improvements in the reputation of self-publishing, some readers and industry professionals still hold biases against self-published books. Overcoming the stigma and proving the quality and value of self-published works can be a significant challenge. 27

9. **Finding Professional Support**: Indie authors often lack the support network and resources provided by traditional publishers, such as professional editors, cover designers, and marketing experts. Finding affordable and reliable professionals to help with various aspects of publishing can be a challenge. 30

10. **Discoverability**: With the vast number of books being published every day, standing out and getting noticed can be a significant challenge for indie authors. Cutting through the noise and making an impact in a crowded market requires strategic marketing, word-of-mouth recommendations, and building a strong online presence. 33

About the Author 36

More Books by the Author 37

1
Finding Your Audience

A Guide for Indie Authors

As an indie author, you've poured your heart and soul into your manuscript. You've meticulously crafted your story, polished your prose, and now you're ready to share your literary creation with the world. But there's one significant challenge standing between you and your readers: finding your audience. In a publishing landscape dominated by traditional publishing houses, indie authors often face the daunting task of reaching and connecting with their target readership. In this blog, we'll explore the intricacies of this challenge and provide you with valuable insights and strategies to help you overcome it.

The Challenge of Finding Your Audience: The world of publishing is vast, with millions of books available in various genres. Readers have countless options to choose from, making it essential for authors to not only write engaging stories but also effectively reach their intended audience. However, indie authors face unique challenges in this endeavor:

1. **Limited Visibility**: Unlike authors backed by traditional publishing houses, indie authors don't benefit from the extensive marketing and distribution networks that major publishers offer. This limited visibility can make it challenging to stand out in a crowded marketplace.
2. **Budget Constraints**: Many indie authors operate on tight budgets, which can restrict their ability to invest in extensive advertising and promotional campaigns. Traditional publishers often have more financial resources to allocate to marketing efforts.

3. **Lack of Established Platforms**: Established publishers often have platforms and connections within the industry that can help them reach readers through bookstores, libraries, and literary events. Indie authors must work harder to establish these connections.

Strategies for Finding Your Audience: While the challenges are real, there are effective strategies that indie authors can employ to connect with their target audience:

1. **Define Your Ideal Reader**: Start by identifying your ideal reader. What are their interests, preferences, and reading habits? Understanding your audience on a deep level will help you tailor your marketing efforts.
2. **Utilize Social Media**: Leverage the power of social media platforms to engage with potential readers. Create author profiles on platforms like Facebook, Twitter, Instagram, and Goodreads to connect with your audience directly.
3. **Content Marketing**: Start a blog or author website where you can share content related to your book's genre or themes. This can help you attract readers who are interested in your subject matter.
4. **Email Marketing**: Build an email list of interested readers and engage with them through newsletters. This allows you to maintain a direct line of communication with your audience.
5. **Book Communities**: Join online book communities and forums related to your genre. Engage in discussions, share your expertise, and subtly promote your work when relevant.
6. **Book Reviews**: Seek book bloggers and reviewers who specialize in your genre. Positive reviews from respected sources can boost your credibility and attract readers.
7. **Collaborate with Other Authors**: Partner with other indie authors for cross-promotion. Collaborative efforts can expand your reach.
8. **Attend Literary Events**: Whenever possible, attend book fairs, conventions, and literary events to connect with readers, fellow authors, and potential reviewers.

Finding your audience as an indie author may be a challenge, but it's a challenge worth embracing. By understanding your ideal reader, leveraging digital tools and platforms, and actively engaging with book communities, you can establish a connection with your target audience. Remember that building a readership takes time, dedication, and a genuine passion for your craft. Stay persistent, keep refining your approach, and your audience will grow, one reader at a time.

2
Limited Marketing Resources:

Strategies for Indie Authors with Limited Resources

Being an indie author comes with many rewards, such as creative freedom and control over your work. However, it also presents unique challenges, one of the most significant being limited marketing resources. Unlike authors backed by traditional publishers, indie authors often operate on tight budgets, making it crucial to find cost-effective yet impactful ways to promote their books. In this blog, we'll delve into the world of marketing for indie authors and explore strategies that can help you make the most of your limited resources.

The Challenge of Limited Marketing Resources: Limited financial resources can be a daunting obstacle for indie authors. Traditional publishing houses often invest substantial budgets in marketing and promotion, including book tours, advertisements, and distribution. Indie authors, on the other hand, must be resourceful and creative in their marketing endeavors. Here are some common challenges:

1. **Budget Constraints**: Indie authors typically lack the financial resources for large-scale advertising and promotional campaigns.
2. **Limited Access to Bookstores**: Major bookstore chains may be reluctant to carry self-published books, limiting physical distribution opportunities.
3. **Competition**: The digital marketplace is crowded, making it challenging to stand out among the millions of books available online.

Strategies for Effective Marketing with Limited Resources: While the challenges are real, indie authors can employ several effective strategies to maximize their marketing efforts without breaking the bank:

1. **Define Your Target Audience**: Understanding your ideal readers is essential. Focus your marketing efforts on reaching the audience most likely to resonate with your book.
2. **Leverage Social Media**: Social media platforms like Facebook, Twitter, Instagram, and Pinterest offer free or low-cost ways to engage with your audience. Consistent and authentic engagement can help build a loyal following.
3. **Content Marketing**: Start a blog or author website where you can share valuable content related to your book's themes, genre, or background research. Regularly updated content can attract readers interested in your subject matter.
4. **Email Marketing**: Build an email list of interested readers and send out newsletters with updates, book launches, and exclusive content. Email marketing is a cost-effective way to maintain direct communication.
5. **Book Blogs and Reviewers**: Identify book bloggers and reviewers who specialize in your genre. Reach out to them for reviews or interviews. Positive reviews can boost your book's credibility.
6. **Online Book Communities**: Join and engage in online book communities, forums, and discussion groups relevant to your genre. Avoid overt self-promotion but participate in discussions and contribute your expertise.
7. **Collaborate with Other Authors**: Partner with other indie authors for cross-promotion. Collaborative efforts can help you expand your reach and pool resources for joint marketing initiatives.
8. **Utilize Free Promotion Days**: If you publish through platforms like Amazon Kindle Direct Publishing (KDP), take advantage of free promotion days or Kindle Countdown Deals to boost visibility.
9. **Book Events and Virtual Launches**: Host virtual book launch events, webinars, or social media takeovers to create

excitement around your book. These events can be cost-effective and reach a global audience.

Limited marketing resources should not deter indie authors from pursuing their publishing dreams. With creativity, determination, and a strategic approach, you can effectively promote your work and connect with your target readership. The key is to be authentic, engage with your audience, and make the most of the affordable yet powerful tools and platforms available in the digital age. Remember, success in indie publishing is often a marathon, not a sprint, so stay committed to your craft and your readers, and your efforts will bear fruit over time.

3
Building Credibility as an Indie Author

Your Path to Trust and Success

For indie authors, the path to success often includes overcoming unique challenges. One of the most significant hurdles is building credibility in a landscape where traditional publishing houses often garner greater trust. Without the stamp of approval from a well-established publisher, indie authors must take proactive steps to gain readers' trust and establish themselves as reputable writers. In this blog, we'll explore strategies to help indie authors build credibility, earn reader trust, and thrive in the competitive world of self-publishing.

The Challenge of Credibility: The absence of traditional publishing backing can create skepticism among readers. They may wonder about the quality and professionalism of self-published works. Overcoming this credibility gap is essential for indie authors who want their books to be taken seriously. Here are some common challenges:

1. **Lack of Validation**: Traditional publishers act as gatekeepers, selecting manuscripts they believe will succeed. Indie authors face skepticism because their works have not undergone this vetting process.
2. **Reader Trust**: Gaining the trust of readers who are wary of self-published books can be challenging. Credibility issues can impact sales and visibility.
3. **Quality Concerns**: Readers may question the quality of self-published books, including editing, formatting, and cover design.

Strategies to Build Credibility: Building credibility is a gradual process that requires persistence, dedication, and a commitment to delivering high-quality work. Here are strategies to help indie authors establish themselves as credible writers:

1. **Professional Editing**: Invest in professional editing services to ensure your manuscript is free from errors and polished to perfection. A well-edited book demonstrates your commitment to quality.
2. **Stellar Cover Design**: Engage a professional cover designer to create an eye-catching and genre-appropriate book cover. A professionally designed cover signals that your book is worth exploring.
3. **Consistent Branding**: Develop a strong author brand that reflects your style, genre, and values. Consistent branding across your website, social media profiles, and book covers helps readers recognize and trust your work.
4. **Engage with Readers**: Actively engage with your readers through social media, email newsletters, and book-related events. Respond to their questions and feedback promptly and courteously.
5. **Build an Author Website**: Create a professional author website where readers can learn more about you and your books. Showcase your portfolio, share your writing journey, and offer valuable content related to your genre or expertise.
6. **Positive Reviews and Endorsements**: Encourage readers to leave honest reviews of your books on platforms like Amazon and Goodreads. Positive reviews and endorsements from other authors can significantly boost your credibility.
7. **Consistent Publishing**: Maintain a consistent publishing schedule to demonstrate your commitment to your writing career. Regularly releasing new works can help build your author brand.
8. **Professional Formatting**: Ensure your book is professionally formatted for both print and digital formats. A

well-formatted book enhances the reading experience and reflects your professionalism.
9. **Book Awards and Competitions**: Consider entering your books in reputable book awards and competitions. Winning or even being recognized as a finalist can boost your credibility.
10. **Author Events and Workshops**: Participate in author events, book signings, and workshops to connect with readers and fellow authors. These activities can help you network and build credibility within the writing community.

While the journey to building credibility as an indie author may be challenging, it's also incredibly rewarding. By investing in professional services, engaging with readers, and consistently delivering high-quality content, you can overcome the initial skepticism and establish yourself as a trusted author. Building credibility is not only about earning the trust of readers but also about believing in the value of your own work. With perseverance and a commitment to your craft, you can thrive in the competitive world of self-publishing and find success on your terms.

4
Quality Control in Self-Publishing

Crafting Professional Books

Self-publishing offers indie authors the freedom to bring their stories and ideas to life without the need for traditional publishing houses. However, with this independence comes a significant responsibility: quality control. Indie authors must wear many hats, including those of editors, proofreaders, and formatters, to ensure their books meet high standards. In this blog, we'll delve into the importance of quality control in self-publishing and provide guidance on how authors can achieve professional results.
The Challenge of Quality Control: Self-published authors face unique challenges when it comes to maintaining quality throughout the publishing process:

1. **Editing**: Without the support of professional editors, authors may overlook grammar, spelling, and structural issues in their manuscripts. These errors can negatively impact the reading experience and damage an author's reputation.
2. **Proofreading**: Even the most skilled writers can miss typos and other mistakes in their work. Proofreading is essential to catch those last-minute errors that editing might have missed.
3. **Formatting**: Formatting plays a crucial role in the presentation of a book. Poor formatting can lead to readability issues, distracting the reader from the story.
4. **Consistency**: Maintaining consistency in style, tone, and formatting throughout the book is vital for a professional look and feel.
5. **Reader Experience**: Ultimately, quality control is about delivering the best possible reading experience to your

audience. Readers expect well-crafted books, and self-published authors must meet these expectations to compete in the market.

Strategies for Quality Control: Achieving professional quality in self-publishing is not impossible. Here are strategies to help authors maintain high standards:

1. **Professional Editing**: Invest in professional editing services to review your manuscript for grammar, syntax, plot holes, and overall coherence. Editing is the foundation of quality control.
2. **Beta Readers**: Enlist beta readers to provide feedback on your manuscript. Their fresh perspective can help uncover issues that you might have missed.
3. **Proofreading**: After editing, hire a proofreader to catch typos, punctuation errors, and any remaining mistakes. Proofreading should be the final step before publication.
4. **Formatting Guides**: Familiarize yourself with formatting guides for both print and digital books. Tools like Amazon's Kindle Create can help with ebook formatting.
5. **Style Guide**: Develop a style guide for your book that includes guidelines for consistency in formatting, punctuation, and style throughout the manuscript.
6. **Read Aloud**: Read your book aloud or use text-to-speech software to identify awkward sentences or errors in flow.
7. **Professional Cover Design**: Your book's cover is its first impression. Invest in professional cover design to ensure it stands out and reflects the book's content.
8. **Author Platform**: Build a strong author platform to connect with readers and receive feedback. Engage with your audience through social media and author websites.
9. **Self-Publishing Communities**: Join self-publishing communities and forums to learn from other authors' experiences and gain insights into quality control.

10. **Quality over Speed**: While it's essential to publish regularly, prioritize quality over speed. Rushed publishing can lead to avoidable errors.

Quality control is an indispensable aspect of self-publishing. To craft professional books that captivate readers, indie authors must invest time, effort, and resources into editing, proofreading, and formatting. While it may require a significant commitment, the result is worth it: books that shine with professionalism and offer readers a top-tier reading experience. By focusing on quality control, indie authors can build their reputations, gain reader trust, and succeed in the competitive world of self-publishing.

5
Navigating Distribution Challenges

Bringing Self-Published Books to Bookstores

Self-publishing empowers authors to share their stories and ideas with the world independently. However, one of the significant challenges faced by self-published authors is distribution, especially when it comes to getting their books into brick-and-mortar bookstores. Many physical stores tend to favor books from established publishing houses, making it difficult for indie authors to secure shelf space. In this blog, we'll explore the distribution challenges that self-published authors encounter and offer strategies to increase visibility and availability in bookstores.

The Challenge of Distribution: Distribution remains a formidable obstacle for self-published authors:

1. **Established Publisher Bias**: Brick-and-mortar bookstores often prioritize books from well-known publishing houses, as they believe these books have a built-in readership and are less risky investments.
2. **Limited Shelf Space**: Bookstores have limited physical shelf space, and competition for these spots is fierce. They prioritize titles with proven sales records and wide recognition.
3. **Return Policies**: Bookstores have strict return policies that can be burdensome for self-published authors. Unsold books may need to be returned, which can result in financial losses.
4. **Visibility**: Self-published books are less likely to be featured prominently or receive prime shelf space, making them harder for customers to discover.

Strategies for Overcoming Distribution Challenges: While the distribution landscape can be challenging for self-published authors, there are several strategies to improve visibility and availability in bookstores:

1. **Online Retailers**: Leverage online retailers like Amazon, Barnes & Noble, and indie bookstores with online platforms. Establishing a strong online presence can drive sales and attract the attention of physical bookstores.
2. **Local Bookstores**: Approach local independent bookstores in your area. They may be more willing to support local authors and offer shelf space for your books.
3. **Consignment Agreements**: Some bookstores accept books on consignment, meaning they only pay for the books that sell. This reduces the financial risk for both the author and the store.
4. **Author Events**: Organize book signings, readings, or author events at local bookstores. This not only increases the visibility of your book but also fosters a relationship with the store.
5. **Book Distributors**: Consider working with book distributors that specialize in independent and self-published titles. They have established relationships with bookstores and can help get your book on their radar.
6. **Professional Packaging**: Ensure your book has a professionally designed cover, high-quality printing, and proper formatting. A polished appearance can help convince bookstores to stock your book.
7. **Metadata Optimization**: Optimize the metadata for your book, including keywords, categories, and descriptions. Accurate and relevant metadata can improve discoverability.
8. **Reader Reviews**: Encourage readers to leave reviews on platforms like Amazon. Positive reviews can enhance your book's credibility and attractiveness to bookstores.
9. **Local Media**: Get coverage in local newspapers, magazines, or on local radio and television. Media exposure can generate interest from local bookstores.

10. **Persistence**: Be persistent and patient. Building relationships with bookstores and gaining their trust may take time. Keep reaching out and promoting your book.

While distribution challenges can be daunting for self-published authors, they are not insurmountable. By adopting a strategic approach, building a strong online presence, and actively engaging with local bookstores and distributors, indie authors can increase the visibility and availability of their books in physical bookstores. Remember that persistence, professionalism, and proactive marketing efforts can help self-published authors overcome distribution obstacles and expand their readership through both online and offline channels.

6
Navigating Financial Challenges as an Indie Author

Strategies for Success

For many aspiring writers, self-publishing offers a path to sharing their stories and ideas with the world. However, one of the most significant challenges faced by indie authors is managing the financial aspects of publishing. Unlike traditional authors who receive advances and extensive support from publishing houses, self-published authors bear the costs of editing, cover design, marketing, and other expenses. This blog explores the financial considerations that indie authors must grapple with and provides strategies for achieving financial sustainability, even as a new or lesser-known author.
The Financial Challenges of Self-Publishing: Self-publishing comes with several financial hurdles that authors must address:

1. **Upfront Costs**: Indie authors are responsible for funding various aspects of publishing, including editing, cover design, formatting, and book printing or digital conversion. These upfront costs can be substantial.
2. **Marketing Expenses**: Promoting a book effectively often requires financial investment in strategies such as advertising, book reviews, social media campaigns, and website development.
3. **Distribution Costs**: Self-published authors may need to allocate resources to ensure their books are available through multiple distribution channels, both online and offline.
4. **Professional Services**: Hiring professional editors, proofreaders, cover designers, and marketing experts can be expensive but is crucial for producing a high-quality book.

5. **Income Uncertainty**: Generating sufficient income from book sales can be uncertain, particularly for new and lesser-known authors who are building their readership.

Strategies for Financial Sustainability: While the financial challenges of self-publishing are real, there are effective strategies to help indie authors achieve financial sustainability:

1. **Budget Wisely**: Create a detailed budget that outlines all expenses related to your book, including editing, cover design, and marketing. Prioritize essential services while being mindful of your overall spending.
2. **Crowdfunding**: Consider using crowdfunding platforms to raise funds for your book project. Engage your readers and offer them exclusive incentives, such as signed copies or personalized content, in exchange for their support.
3. **DIY Approach**: Learn basic editing, formatting, and design skills to handle some tasks yourself and reduce outsourcing costs. However, ensure that quality is not compromised.
4. **Hybrid Publishing**: Explore hybrid publishing models that combine self-publishing and traditional publishing. These models may provide financial support and expertise while allowing authors to retain creative control.
5. **Financial Planning**: Set realistic financial goals for your book project. Understand that it may take time to recoup your initial investments, and long-term financial planning is crucial.
6. **Collaboration**: Partner with other authors for joint marketing efforts or co-authored projects to share costs and reach a broader audience.
7. **Professional Services**: Invest in professional services selectively. Prioritize editing and cover design, as these elements significantly impact your book's quality and marketability.
8. **Build an Author Platform**: Focus on building a strong author platform through social media, a website, and email

marketing. A well-established online presence can help sell books without extensive advertising costs.
9. **Leverage Free Promotion**: Utilize free or low-cost promotional methods, such as social media engagement, guest blogging, and participation in book-related communities.
10. **Diversify Income Streams**: Consider diversifying your income streams by offering related products or services, such as online courses or merchandise, that align with your book's themes.

While the financial challenges of self-publishing can be daunting, they should not deter aspiring authors from pursuing their dreams. With careful financial planning, strategic budgeting, and a commitment to quality, indie authors can overcome these obstacles and achieve financial sustainability. Remember that building an author brand and steadily growing your readership are long-term endeavors that can lead to increased book sales and financial success. By adopting a proactive and financially savvy approach, indie authors can navigate the world of self-publishing while managing their resources effectively.

7
Mastering Time Management for Self-Published Authors

The journey of a self-published author is often likened to wearing multiple hats. You're not just the writer; you're the editor, marketer, distributor, and more. While this level of control is empowering, it can also be overwhelming, especially when you have other commitments and obligations in your life. In this blog, we'll explore effective time management strategies for self-published authors, helping you strike a balance between your writing career and other responsibilities.

The Challenges of Time Management in Self-Publishing: Self-published authors face several challenges when it comes to managing their time effectively:

1. **Multifaceted Roles**: Authors must juggle various roles, such as writing, editing, cover design, marketing, and distribution. Each of these tasks demands time and attention.
2. **Limited Hours**: Like everyone else, authors have a finite number of hours in a day. Balancing writing and publishing with work, family, and personal life can be a Herculean task.
3. **Deadlines**: Meeting self-imposed deadlines for writing, editing, and publishing can be stressful, especially when life's unexpected events come into play.
4. **Marketing and Promotion**: Effective book promotion often requires ongoing effort, such as social media engagement, email marketing, and interacting with readers, which can be time-consuming.
5. **Avoiding Burnout**: Authors must guard against burnout, which can result from overworking and neglecting self-care.

Effective Time Management Strategies: To successfully manage your time as a self-published author, consider these strategies:

1. **Set Clear Goals**: Define your writing and publishing goals. Knowing what you want to achieve will help you prioritize tasks effectively.
2. **Create a Schedule**: Develop a daily or weekly schedule that allocates time for writing, editing, marketing, and other essential tasks. Stick to your schedule as closely as possible.
3. **Prioritize Tasks**: Identify high-priority tasks and tackle them first. Focus on activities that directly contribute to your writing and publishing goals.
4. **Time Blocking**: Use time-blocking techniques to allocate specific time slots for different activities. For example, reserve mornings for writing and afternoons for marketing.
5. **Use Productivity Tools**: Utilize productivity apps and tools to help manage your time, set reminders, and track your progress.
6. **Outsource When Possible**: Consider outsourcing tasks that you aren't skilled in or that are particularly time-consuming, such as cover design or formatting.
7. **Set Realistic Deadlines**: Establish achievable deadlines for writing, editing, and publishing. Avoid overloading your schedule with unrealistic expectations.
8. **Batch Tasks**: Group similar tasks together and tackle them in batches. For instance, schedule a block of time for social media posts or email marketing.
9. **Learn to Say No**: Be selective about commitments outside of your writing career. Politely decline activities or events that don't align with your priorities.
10. **Take Breaks**: Schedule regular breaks to recharge and prevent burnout. Short, frequent breaks can boost productivity and creativity.
11. **Track Your Time**: Keep a record of how you spend your time. This can help you identify areas where you can become more efficient.

12. **Flexibility**: Allow for some flexibility in your schedule to accommodate unexpected events or creative inspiration.

Effective time management is crucial for self-published authors striving to balance their writing career with other life responsibilities. By setting clear goals, prioritizing tasks, and using time management strategies tailored to your needs, you can navigate the multifaceted world of self-publishing while maintaining a healthy work-life balance. Remember that mastering time management is an ongoing process, and with practice, you'll become more efficient and productive in your writing journey.

8
Breaking Boundaries

Overcoming Stigma in Self-Publishing

The landscape of publishing has evolved significantly in recent years, with self-publishing emerging as a viable and respected avenue for authors to share their stories with the world. However, despite the notable progress in the reputation of self-publishing, a stigma still persists among some readers and industry professionals. In this blog, we'll explore the challenges posed by this stigma and strategies to overcome it while proving the quality and value of self-published works.

Understanding the Stigma: The stigma associated with self-publishing primarily stems from misconceptions and historical biases:

1. **Quality Concerns**: Some assume that self-published books lack the quality, editing, and polish often associated with traditionally published works.
2. **Vanity Press Associations**: The historical association with vanity presses, which produced low-quality books for authors willing to pay, still lingers in the industry's memory.
3. **Volume Overload**: The sheer volume of self-published books available can make it challenging for readers to sift through and find quality content.
4. **Negative Reviews**: A few poorly reviewed or unedited self-published books can contribute to a negative perception of the entire self-publishing industry.

Overcoming the Stigma:

1. **Professionalism is Key**: Invest in professional editing, cover design, and formatting. Presenting a polished product will counter assumptions of low quality.
2. **Engage Beta Readers**: Enlist beta readers to provide constructive feedback before publishing. Their insights can help you refine your work.
3. **Authenticity**: Be transparent about your self-publishing journey. Share your commitment to producing quality work and your reasons for choosing self-publishing.
4. **Strong Online Presence**: Establish a strong online presence through an author website and active engagement on social media. Showcase your dedication to your craft and connect with your audience.
5. **Positive Reviews**: Encourage genuine readers to leave positive reviews. Quality reviews can offset the impact of negative stereotypes.
6. **Networking**: Connect with fellow authors, both self-published and traditionally published. Building relationships within the writing community can help dispel biases.
7. **Professional Book Covers**: Invest in professionally designed book covers that capture the essence of your work and reflect its quality.
8. **Consistency**: Publish multiple books to demonstrate your commitment to your craft and to dispel the notion that self-published authors produce a single work and disappear.
9. **Engage in Industry Events**: Attend writing conferences, book fairs, and industry events to network and learn from professionals. This shows your dedication to growth and improvement.
10. **Quality Control**: Take pride in your work by adhering to high-quality standards in all aspects of publishing.

While overcoming the stigma associated with self-publishing may be challenging, it's not insurmountable. By consistently delivering high-quality content, engaging with your readers and peers, and actively working to counter negative perceptions, you can prove the quality and value of self-published works. Remember that the self-publishing landscape continues to evolve, and with each new success story, the stigma diminishes, making way for the recognition and respect that self-published authors deserve.

9
Navigating the Indie Author's Journey

Finding Professional Support

The world of independent publishing, often referred to as indie publishing, has witnessed a remarkable surge in recent years. With the advent of digital platforms and self-publishing tools, authors now have unprecedented opportunities to bring their literary creations to the world. However, this newfound freedom also comes with its unique set of challenges, particularly when it comes to securing professional support. Indie authors often lack the extensive support networks and resources that traditional publishers offer, including access to professional editors, cover designers, and marketing experts. In this blog, we'll explore the importance of finding professional support for indie authors and offer insights into how to navigate this crucial aspect of your publishing journey.

The Indie Author's Journey: Indie authors embark on a solitary journey, one that requires not only creative storytelling but also proficiency in various other areas of publishing. Unlike traditional authors, who often have a team of professionals at their disposal, indie authors must wear multiple hats, acting as writers, publishers, marketers, and more. While this level of control can be empowering, it also underscores the need for professional support to ensure the final product meets industry standards.

The Role of Professional Editors: One of the critical aspects of publishing a book is ensuring its quality. Professional editors play a pivotal role in refining an author's work, identifying errors, improving readability, and enhancing overall storytelling. However, finding an editor who is both affordable and reliable can be a daunting task for indie authors. Researching and vetting potential editors is essential to establish a productive and collaborative working relationship.

Crafting an Eye-Catching Cover: A book's cover is often the first thing that catches a reader's eye. It should not only be visually appealing but also convey the essence of the story within. Designing a captivating cover requires the expertise of a skilled graphic designer, another professional often beyond the reach of indie authors. However, there are cost-effective solutions, such as hiring freelance designers or using reputable self-publishing platforms that offer cover design services.

Navigating the Marketing Maze: Marketing a book is an art and science in itself. It involves building an author brand, reaching out to potential readers, and creating buzz around your work. Traditional publishers have dedicated marketing teams, but indie authors must often take the reins themselves or seek outside help. Professional marketers can assist in crafting effective marketing strategies tailored to your book's target audience, optimizing your chances of success.

Tips for Finding Affordable and Reliable Professionals:
    a. **Network within Writing Communities:** Engage with fellow authors, both indie and traditionally published, to seek recommendations for editors, designers, and marketers.
    b. **Online Freelance Platforms:** Platforms like Upwork and Fiverr offer a wide range of freelancers, allowing you to browse portfolios and reviews to find suitable professionals.
    c. **Industry Associations:** Organizations like the Editorial Freelancers Association (EFA) or the Association of Authors' Representatives (AAR) can provide lists of vetted professionals.
    d. **Online Writing Groups:** Join online communities and forums where authors share their experiences and connect with professionals who offer their services at competitive rates.
    e. **Interview and Collaborate:** Don't hesitate to interview potential professionals, ask for samples of their work, and discuss your project's specific needs before making a commitment.

The journey of an indie author is filled with both creative fulfillment and entrepreneurial challenges. Finding professional support is a critical step in ensuring your work meets the high standards of the publishing industry. While it may require extra effort to discover affordable and reliable professionals, the investment in your book's quality and success is well worth it. As you embark on your indie author journey, remember that you're not alone—there's a vast community of professionals and fellow authors ready to support you every step of the way.

10
Navigating the Indie Author's Challenge

Discoverability in a Crowded Market

The indie author's journey is an exhilarating one, filled with creative freedom and the thrill of bringing stories to life. However, there's a formidable challenge that all indie authors face: discoverability. In an era where countless books are published daily, getting noticed amidst the literary noise is no small feat. This blog explores the significance of discoverability for indie authors and provides insights into
strategies for standing out in a crowded market.

The Overwhelming Sea of Books: The digital age has democratized publishing, allowing authors to bypass traditional gatekeepers and share their work directly with readers. While this has opened up exciting opportunities, it has also led to an exponential increase in the number of books available. The result is a literary marketplace flooded with options, making it harder for any single book to gain recognition.

The Role of Discoverability: Discoverability is the process by which readers find and engage with new books and authors. It encompasses everything from online searches and bookstore recommendations to word-of-mouth referrals and social media buzz. In essence, discoverability is the bridge that connects authors with their potential audience.

Crafting a Strong Online Presence: In the digital age, having a robust online presence is a fundamental aspect of discoverability. This includes maintaining an author website, engaging with readers on social media, and utilizing platforms like Goodreads and

Amazon Author Central. By consistently sharing content related to your writing journey, insights, and book updates, you can create a community of engaged readers.

Leveraging Social Media: Social media platforms offer a dynamic space for authors to connect with readers, fellow writers, and book enthusiasts. Engage authentically with your audience, share snippets of your work, and participate in conversations relevant to your genre or niche. Platforms like Twitter, Instagram, Facebook, and TikTok can be powerful tools for building your author brand.

The Importance of Strategic Marketing: Effective marketing is essential for gaining visibility in a crowded market. Develop a comprehensive marketing plan that includes book launches, promotions, and collaborations with book bloggers and influencers. Email marketing campaigns can help you reach your existing readers and keep them engaged.

Harnessing the Power of Reviews: Reader reviews can significantly impact discoverability. Encourage your readers to leave reviews on platforms like Amazon and Goodreads. Authentic, positive reviews can attract new readers and build trust in your work.

Word-of-Mouth Recommendations: Word-of-mouth remains one of the most potent drivers of discoverability. Encourage your readers to recommend your books to friends and family. Consider joining book clubs or online reading communities where passionate readers discuss their favorite titles.

Niche and Genre Communities: Identify and engage with niche or genre-specific communities and forums. These spaces often have dedicated readers who are actively seeking new authors and books within their preferred genres.

Embrace the Long Game: Building discoverability is not an overnight achievement. It's a gradual process that requires patience and perseverance. Consistently delivering high-quality content and engaging with your readership will yield long-term benefits.

Discoverability is the cornerstone of an indie author's success in today's crowded literary landscape. While it may seem daunting, it's a challenge that can be met with strategic marketing, a strong online presence, and the support of your readers.

Remember that every successful indie author started somewhere, and by continuously refining your approach to discoverability, you can navigate the crowded market and find your place among the literary stars.

About the Author

B Alan Bourgeois began his writing career at the age of 12, writing screenplays for the Adam-12 show. Despite not submitting them for review, this experience sparked his passion for writing. However, he followed the advice of his generation and pursued higher education to secure a stable job. It wasn't until 1989, after taking a writing class at a community college, that Bourgeois wrote a short story that was published. Since then, he has written over 48 short stories and published more than 10 books, including the award-winning spiritual thriller "Extinguishing the Light."

Bourgeois has become a champion for authors and founded the Texas Authors Association in 2011 to help Texas authors better market and sell their books. This led to the creation of the Texas Authors Institute of History, Inc., and the first online museum of its kind, the Texas Authors Institute. He also created several short story contests and fundraising programs for Texas students and consolidated small-town book festivals into the Lone Star Festival, promoting Texas authors, musicians, artists, and filmmakers. In 2016, he founded the Authors Marketing Event and added a Certification program in 2017, allowing attendees to gain accreditation for their hard work in learning book marketing. His recent focus has been on assisting authors of all levels to become successful Authorpreneurs through the Authors School of Business, which offers programs to help grow their careers. He is currently working with NFTs for authors to help them increase their income channels.

Top Ten Book Series and Other Books by the Author

Available at Your Favorite Bookstore

100+ Questions a Writer/Author Should Ask

Looking to take your writing career to the next level? Look no further than "100+ Questions a Writer/Author Should Ask"! With over 100 questions curated by Award-Winning Author & Speaker B Alan Bourgeois, the founder and CEO of the Authors School of Business, this book is a must-have for any aspiring or established writer. Bourgeois, a seasoned publisher, author advocate, and educator, brings his wealth of experience to the table to help you better understand the publishing world and succeed in your career. Don't miss out on this valuable resource.

Top Ten Mistakes Authors Make when Creating a Book Cover

Your book cover is your first impression. Don't let a lackluster design hold you back. "Top Ten Mistakes Authors Make When Creating a Book Cover" is your comprehensive guide to avoid common pitfalls and create a cover that truly represents your work. Discover practical tips on how to choose the right colors, fonts, and design, and avoid using low-quality images and cluttered layouts. With real-world examples and expert advice, this book will help you create a cover that grabs readers' attention and leads to more sales.

Don't let a poorly designed book cover hold you back from success. Whether you're self-publishing or working with a traditional publisher, "Top Ten Mistakes Authors Make When Creating a Book Cover" is a must-read. Order your copy today and take your book to the next level!

Top Ten Things to Consider for a Great Sales Pitch

Are you struggling to create a sales pitch that really resonates with your audience? Look no further than "Top Ten Things to Consider for a Great Sales Pitch"! This ultimate guide will take you through the ten most important steps to creating a sales pitch that will grab your target audience's attention and convince them to buy your book.

Learn how to identify your target audience and highlight the unique value of your book, using emotional language to connect with readers on a personal level. Be concise and to the point, and practice your pitch until you can deliver it smoothly and confidently. Incorporate social proof and visuals to make your pitch more compelling, and tailor it to the specific interests and needs of your audience.

Above all, be authentic and genuine. With the help of "Top Ten Things to Consider for a Great Sales Pitch", you'll be able to create a sales pitch that not only sells your book, but also connects with your audience and builds a loyal fan base. Don't miss out on this essential resource for any author looking to take their sales pitch to the next level!

Top Ten Publishing Issues Authors Deal With

Are you an aspiring author struggling with the daunting publishing process? Look no further than "Top Ten Publishing Issues Authors Deal With." This essential guide tackles the most common challenges writers face, including rejection, editing, marketing, distribution, audience building, time management, and legal issues like copyright infringement. Our expert advice will help you navigate the complex world of publishing and achieve success. Plus, we'll guide you through the formatting process, even for ebooks that need to work on multiple devices and software. Don't let self-doubt and imposter syndrome hinder your progress - get the knowledge you need to thrive in the publishing world. Order your copy of "Top Ten Publishing Issues Authors Deal With" today.

Top Ten Marketing Materials an Author Should Use

"Top Ten Marketing Items Authors Should Use" is the ultimate guide for authors who want to boost book sales and increase visibility. Discover the top ten marketing materials every author should use, including eye-catching bookmarks, business cards, posters, and book trailers. You'll also learn insider tips on how to write an attention-grabbing press release and build an author website that attracts readers and media attention. Plus, social media marketing, author blogging, email newsletters, and swag creation strategies will help you connect with readers, build your author brand, and create a loyal fan base. Don't let your book languish in obscurity - get your copy of "Top Ten Marketing Items Authors Should Use" today and take the first step towards successful book promotion!

Top Ten Mistakes an Author Makes Marketing Their Books

Are you an author struggling to make a name for yourself in the crowded world of book marketing? Do you want to avoid the most common mistakes that authors make when promoting their books? Then look no further than "Top 10 Mistakes Authors Make Marketing Their Books" by B Alan Bourgeois.

As an award-winning author and author advocate with years of experience in the publishing industry, Bourgeois has seen it all when it comes to book marketing. In this insightful guide, he shares the top 10 mistakes that authors make and provides practical advice on how to avoid them.

Whether you're a first-time author or a seasoned pro, "Top 10 Mistakes Authors Make Marketing Their Books" is the essential guide for taking your book marketing to the next level. With Bourgeois's expert guidance, you'll learn how to identify your target audience, build a strong online presence, engage with readers, and leverage book reviews to increase sales.

Don't let common marketing mistakes hold you back from the success you deserve. Get your copy of "Top 10 Mistakes Authors Make Marketing Their Books" today and start marketing your book like a pro!

Top Ten Mistakes Authors Make During an Interview

Are you tired of stumbling through interviews, leaving the audience uninterested and disengaged? Do you struggle with staying focused and concise when answering tough questions? Look no further!

Our book provides you with the top ten mistakes authors commonly make at interviews and gives you practical tips on how to avoid them. From preparing adequately by researching the interviewer and their audience, to staying authentic and avoiding complex jargon, we cover it all.

Don't let your lack of enthusiasm or defensiveness turn off your audience. Instead, learn how to show genuine interest in your topic and stay calm during challenging questions. And most importantly, don't forget to thank your interviewer and audience for their time and attention - it can make all the difference in leaving a positive impression.

So, are you ready to improve your interview skills and leave a lasting impact on your audience? Get your copy of "Top Ten Mistakes Authors Do at Interviews" today!

Top Ten Mistakes Authors Make Presenting at Events

Are you an author struggling to present at events? "Top Ten Mistakes Authors Make Presenting at Events" is here to help you avoid common pitfalls and present your best self. Learn how to tailor your presentation to the audience's needs, engage with them effectively, promote your book without being pushy, and more!

With this ultimate guide, you'll avoid going off-topic, losing your audience's attention, and being dull and uninteresting. Practice and rehearse your presentation to deliver it smoothly and confidently. Get your copy of "Top Ten Mistakes Authors Make Presenting at Events" today and make the most of every event you attend!

Top Ten AI Programs Apps Authors Should Use

Attention all writers and authors! Are you looking for ways to improve your writing, stay organized, and streamline your workflow? Look no further than our latest book "Top Ten AI programs/Apps a writer/author should use". In this book, we have compiled a list of the top ten AI programs and apps that will help you with your writing, marketing, and workflow. From Grammarly and ProWritingAid to Hemingway and Dragon Dictation, these programs will help you write a great book.

Although the author has not used all of the programs listed, this list was compiled in 2023 from various sources and provides valuable insight into the most effective AI tools for writers and authors. Keep in mind that the AI community is constantly developing new resources and programs, so this list may not be the most up-to-date.

Don't miss out on the opportunity to improve your writing and streamline your workflow. Order "Top Ten AI programs/Apps a writer/author should use" now and start using these powerful tools to produce your best work.

B Alan Bourgeois

Top Ten Advantages Indie Authors Have Over Traditional Authors

"Top Ten Advantages Indie Authors Have over Traditional" is the ultimate guide for authors looking to take control of their publishing process. With complete control over everything from writing to distribution, independent authors have more flexibility and creative control over their work.

This book highlights the benefits of indie publishing, including higher royalties, faster publishing timelines, the ability to target niche markets, and global distribution through online retailers. If you want more control over your book's content and the ability to reach readers worldwide, "Top Ten Advantages Indie Authors Have over Traditional" is a must-read. Get your copy today and start your journey towards independent publishing success!

Top Ten Pieces of Advice from an Author Advocate & Consultant

"Top Ten Pieces of Advice from an Author Advocate & Consultant" is the ultimate guide for aspiring writers. Learn from an experienced author consultant and advocate and take your writing career to the next level. From building an author platform to developing a marketing plan, this book offers invaluable insights and practical tips to help you achieve your writing goals and make your work stand out. Start your journey to becoming a successful author today by purchasing this must-have resource.

Top Twelve Things to Make the Year of the Indie Authors Great

Are you an indie author looking to make 2024 a great year for your writing career? Then look no further than the book "Top Twelve Things to Make the Year of the Indie Authors Great." This book offers valuable insights into the top 12 things that could make 2024 a great year for indie authors to gain more readers.

With increased acceptance of self-publishing and better distribution channels, indie authors have more options than ever before to reach a wider audience. Additionally, the rise of social media platforms and digital marketing offers affordable ways for authors to connect with readers and promote their work.

But that's not all. The book also covers the importance of collaborating with other authors, the increasing popularity of audiobooks, and the need for more diverse representation in literature. And for those looking to improve their writing skills and production quality, the book offers insights into the better tools and resources available to indie authors.

Finally, the book covers opportunities for indie authors to engage with their readers, showcase their work at book festivals and online events, and collaborate with traditional publishers. In short, "Top Twelve Things to Make the Year of the Indie Authors Great" is a must-read for any indie author looking to take their writing career to the next level in 2024.

Top Ten Steps for a Writers Self-Care

Writing can be an exciting and fulfilling pursuit, but it can also be stressful and overwhelming. As an author, it's important to prioritize your mental and physical health to avoid burnout and ensure longevity in your career. The Writer's Self-Care Handbook provides a comprehensive guide to help you balance your work and personal life, manage stress, and prioritize your well-being.

In this book, you'll discover practical tips and strategies for taking breaks, practicing mindfulness, setting boundaries, staying organized, connecting with others, taking care of your physical health, practicing self-compassion, finding healthy ways to manage stress, taking time for hobbies, and seeking support when needed. Whether you're a seasoned author or just starting out, The Writer's Self-Care Handbook offers valuable insights and advice to help you thrive in your writing career while taking care of yourself. Take the first step towards a healthier, happier writing life by getting your copy today!

Top Ten Steps to Finding the Right Editor

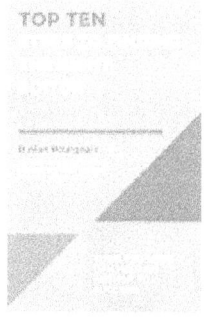

Are you struggling to find the right editor for your writing project? Look no further than "The Author's Guide to Finding and Working with the Right Editor." In this comprehensive guide, we provide the top ten things authors should keep in mind when finding and working with an editor. From determining your editing needs to maintaining a positive relationship with your editor, this guide covers everything you need to know to ensure a successful collaboration. Learn how to research potential editors, check their credentials, communicate clearly, be open to feedback, and more. Whether you're a first-time author or a seasoned pro, this guide is essential for anyone looking to take their writing to the next level with the help of a skilled and trusted editor.

Top Ten Ways to Brand Yourself as an Author

As an author, it's not just enough to write an amazing book. In today's crowded marketplace, building a brand is essential to stand out and make a lasting impression on readers. In "Brand Yourself as an Author," we provide a top ten guide to help you define your brand identity, create a unique logo, develop a consistent visual identity, build a professional website, use social media to promote your brand, create valuable content, leverage email marketing, collaborate with other authors and brands, participate in events and conferences, and stay true to your brand. With our actionable tips, you'll learn how to build a strong and recognizable brand that resonates with your audience and sets you apart in the competitive world of publishing. Don't miss out on this essential guide to building your author brand!

Top Ten Keys for Successful Writing and Productivity

Are you an aspiring writer struggling to make writing a regular habit? Do you need help setting realistic goals and managing your time effectively to achieve success as an author? Look no further than "The Successful Author's Guide to Writing and Productivity." This comprehensive guide offers practical tips on making writing a habit, setting achievable goals, managing your time, focusing on quality, editing and revising, seeking feedback, building an audience, networking, staying organized, and staying motivated. With advice from successful authors, editors, and writing coaches, this book is a must-have for anyone looking to achieve success as an author. Whether you're a new writer or an experienced author looking to take your writing to the next level, "The Successful Author's Guide to Writing and Productivity" will provide you with the tools and techniques you need to achieve your writing goals. Don't wait any longer to become the successful author you've always wanted to be - grab a copy of "The Successful Author's Guide to Writing and Productivity" today!

Top Ten Keys to the Business of Writing

Are you an aspiring or established author struggling with the business side of publishing? Look no further than The Business of Writing: A Comprehensive Guide for Authors. This essential guide provides in-depth information on the top ten items that every author needs to understand, from publishing contracts to managing finances. Learn how to negotiate contract terms, calculate royalties, promote and market your book, build an author platform, and understand copyright laws and intellectual property. You'll also gain insights into the publishing industry, professional networking, and ongoing professional development. With practical advice and expert insights, The Business of Writing is the ultimate resource for authors who want to succeed in the competitive world of publishing.

Top Ten Challenges for Indie/Self-Published Authors

Top Ten Steps to Research Like a Pro

Writing a book can be a daunting task, but conducting research to support your writing can be just as challenging. With "Research Like a Pro: The Ultimate Guide for Writers," you'll learn how to conduct research like a pro, from identifying your research needs to analyzing your findings.

This book provides practical tips on how to use reliable sources, develop a research plan, and organize your materials effectively. You'll learn how to take detailed notes, keep track of citations, and analyze your research to identify patterns and themes.

With "Research Like a Pro," you'll be equipped with the knowledge and tools to effectively use research to support your writing. Whether you're a new writer or a seasoned pro, this book will help you take your research skills to the next level and produce high-quality writing that is well-supported and grounded in evidence.

Top Ten Steps to Market Mastery for Authors

Introducing "Top Ten Steps to Market Mastery for Authors." This comprehensive guide is the key to successfully publishing your book and achieving commercial success. It goes beyond simply writing a book and equips you with the essential knowledge and tools to understand and captivate your target market.

From conducting thorough market research to analyzing sales data, "Market Mastery" covers it all. Discover how to leverage social media effectively, connect with readers at book fairs and conferences, and gain valuable insights through writing groups. Stay ahead of industry trends and developments to keep your book relevant and appealing to your audience.

No matter if you're a first-time author or a seasoned pro, "Market Mastery" will empower you to identify your target audience, understand their preferences, and distinguish your book from competitors. With a strategic marketing approach and willingness to adapt, you'll be on the path to commercial success. Get ready to conquer your target audience and take your writing career to new heights with "Market Mastery."

Top Ten Steps to Creating an Author Platform

Are you an author looking to build your online presence and connect with your readership? Then " Top Ten Steps to Creating an Author Platform " is the perfect resource for you. With practical tips on defining your target audience, establishing a website, creating a blog, building an email list, utilizing social media, attending events and conferences, collaborating with other authors, offering free content, and being consistent, this guide has everything you need to build and maintain a strong author platform. By following the advice of successful authors and marketing experts, you'll learn how to attract readers, establish yourself as an authority in your field, and promote your work effectively. Whether you're a new or experienced author, " Top Ten Steps to Creating an Author Platform " is an essential tool for any writer looking to take their career to the next level. Don't wait any longer to build your online presence - grab a copy today and start building your author platform!

Top Ten Keys to Author Networking

Are you an aspiring author struggling to make industry connections? Are you looking for ways to expand your network and take your writing career to the next level? Look no further than " Top Ten Keys to Author Networking." This comprehensive guide offers practical advice on attending conferences and events, joining writing organizations, connecting on social media, attending book signings and readings, participating in online forums, attending book fairs, joining Twitter pitch parties, reaching out to authors in your genre, and maintaining a professional and polite demeanor. With tips from successful authors and industry professionals, this book is a must-have for any writer looking to make meaningful connections in the publishing world. Don't miss out on the opportunity to expand your network and increase your chances of success - grab a copy of " Top Ten Keys to Author Networking " today!

Top Ten Reasons an Author Should Use NFT and Blockchain

Top Ten Reasons an Author Should Use NFT and Blockchain is packed with invaluable insights and practical advice, this ultimate guide empowers authors on their journey to digital publishing success. Discover compelling reasons to embrace NFTs, from ensuring authenticity and automating royalties to exploring limited editions and global accessibility. Gain essential knowledge on creating NFTs, mastering smart contracts, and navigating legal considerations. Don't miss your chance to create a lasting legacy and tap into the transformative power of NFTs and blockchain. Get your copy today and embark on a journey towards publishing success! Unlock the potential of NFTs and blockchain technology with "Top Ten Reasons an Authors Should Use NFT and Blockchain.

Top Ten Steps to Build an Engaged Reader Community

Top Ten Steps to Build an Engaged Reader Community the ultimate guide for authors who want to connect with their audience and create a supportive network. Learn how to define your target audience, master social media engagement, start a captivating blog, offer exclusive content, interact with readers, host virtual events, collaborate with other authors, create a compelling newsletter, encourage user-generated content, and show appreciation. With proven strategies and practical advice, this book empowers you to cultivate a supportive and enthusiastic community around your writing, propelling your author career to new heights. Don't miss out on this transformative opportunity!

The Non-Fiction Nexus: AI and the Future of Writing

Numerous enterprises have leveraged literary works spanning across eras to steer their Artificial Intelligence down the path of comprehending human existence, with a more distinct focus on crafting top-tier human-like prose. In the realm of education, AI has ingeniously generated an array of refined intellectual compositions. This leads us to ponder: "Should AI replace non-fiction writers?" "The Non-Fiction Nexus: AI and the Future of Writing" delves into both the advantageous and adverse facets of this query, shedding light on the AI perspective. The book explores the current AI landscape in writing, offering a glimpse into the present state and a tantalizing peek into the potential future.

Narrative Nexus: The AI Dilemma in Fiction

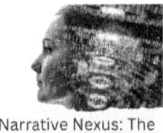

Numerous enterprises have leveraged literary works spanning across eras to steer their Artificial Intelligence down the path of comprehending human existence, with a more distinct focus on crafting top-tier human-like prose. In the realm of education, AI has ingeniously generated an array of refined intellectual compositions. This leads us to ponder: "Should AI replace fictional writers?" "Narrative Nexus: The AI Dilemma in Fiction" delves into both the advantageous and adverse facets of this query, shedding light on the AI perspective. The book explores the current AI landscape in writing, offering a glimpse into the present state and a tantalizing peek into the potential future.

Character Chronicles: Crafting Depth and Consistency in Creative Projects

Are you a creator in literature, film, TV, theater, or gaming? Craft characters that leap off the page and screen! "Character Chronicles" is your ultimate guide to mastering character development.

"Character Chronicles" is more than a book; it's your key to character mastery. Whether you're a pro or a newbie, this resource elevates your storytelling. Don't settle for two-dimensional characters. Enter the world of "Character Chronicles" and breathe life into your creations. Transform your projects with unforgettable characters that captivate your audience. Start your character journey today!

Navigating Amazon Publishing: A Comprehensive Guide for Authors

Are you an aspiring author seeking to publish your work? Amazon offers a wealth of opportunities, but it's essential to navigate this vast platform with a clear understanding of its strengths and potential challenges. In "Navigating Amazon Publishing," we provide you with valuable insights into why many authors choose Amazon and the factors you should weigh before making your decision.

Top Ten Challenges for Indie/Self-Published Authors: Navigating the Road to Success

Are you an indie author determined to thrive in the competitive world of self-publishing? Dive into the invaluable insights offered by "Top Ten Challenges for Indie/Self-Published Authors: Navigating the Road to Success," your essential guide to conquering the hurdles that indie authors face on their publishing journey. From finding your audience and unlocking marketing magic to building credibility and mastering quality control, this comprehensive guide empowers you to navigate the challenges of self-publishing with confidence. Learn to transform financial challenges into opportunities, master time management, defy stigma, and discover the secrets to effective marketing and discoverability. Don't let these challenges hold you back; embrace them as stepping stones toward your indie publishing success. "Top Ten Challenges for Indie/Self-Published Authors" equips you with the knowledge and strategies to conquer these obstacles and emerge as a triumphant indie author. Your journey begins now!

B Alan Bourgeois has an extensive track record of having helped hundreds of authors achieve their publishing goals through a variety of channels, including self-publishing and hybrid models. He is skilled in guiding authors to literary agents that are aligned with their specific needs.

Leveraging his extensive experience in book marketing and sales, as well as his participation in numerous book festivals, library conferences, and writing conferences, B Alan Bourgeois is able to assist authors in identifying and selecting the most suitable events to advance their careers. He further represents his clients at these conferences through his various organizations.

B Alan Bourgeois' consulting services are available to authors at every stage of their writing journeys - from beginners to seasoned professionals seeking new avenues for growth.

If you are interested in benefiting from his expertise, please complete the form below and he will promptly contact you to discuss your needs and how he can assist you. His first 15-minute consultation comes at no charge, and his hourly rate begins at $150 with the added benefit of discounts for purchasing multiple hours at once.

Top Ten Challenges for Indie/Self-Published Authors

It should be noted that the recommended consulting duration for new authors is approximately 3-5 hours, whereas more experienced authors may only require 1/2 hour-2 hours of consultation time.

To schedule a consultation, please visit the authors website at: http://bourgeoismedia.com/index.php/consulting-service/consulting-service-2

Milton Keynes UK
Ingram Content Group UK Ltd.
UKHW020733161023
430697UK00016B/742